# THE ALTHORP ESTATE

My Great Aunt and I are the last two Spencers to have held "Coming of Age" parties at Spencer House; but the bond between us is based on something more tangible than that. She has always been the greatest friend, excellent company, and a mine of information about the myriad figures who hang in their frames at Althorp.

I had always hoped that, one day, she would record some of her earliest memories, for others to enjoy first hand. In this book she has focused on intriguing moments in a childhood played out against the sadness of her motherless state, with her broken Father tragically looming in the background, and a sense of the ending of that age that disappeared with the Great War.

It is all brought to life by the magical eye of a perceptive and indomitably optimistic lady that I am proud to be able to call "Aunt".

*Charles Spencer*

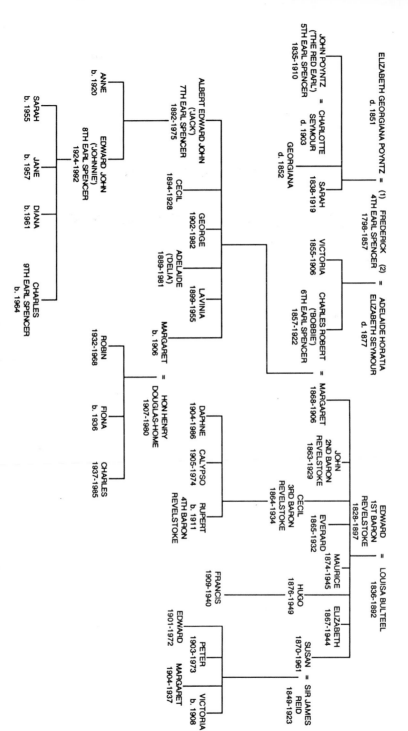

SPENCER

BARING

In memory of my two sons

ROBIN AND CHARLIE DOUGLAS-HOME

"I was born in London in the second half of 1906 - I was not an only child, though it has been difficult, at times, to remember that.

My brothers and sisters were much older and had already left home, to move into a fuller existence.

In this book, I have tried to bring out the unusual atmosphere in which we lived, and the love and appreciation which went with it."

*Margaret Douglas-Home*

# *Preface*

This is a memoir, perhaps a rêverie, a moment of renewed recognition. It is a memory indelibly printed, still vivid, even to the texture of the threadbare carpet along the winding corridor leading to the roof. To remember it brings back the tingling silence gently disrupted by the quarterly chimes of the stable clock. It happened. It is not a fantasy of the mind.

When John Evelyn visited Althorp, Northamptonshire, in 1788, he noted in his Diary "it is a noble uniformed pile". But, for the many Spencers who have lived there since, loving it above all else, Althorp has been much more than that, not least for a little girl, dreaming on the rooftop more than 70 years ago.

The devotees of previous centuries who spring to mind most instantly include Sir John Spencer, who began planting his woodlands in 1567, in one case finishing a plantation without disturbing a long-established 'hernery' nearby. Then there is Robert, second Earl of Sunderland (1640-1702), known as 'The Apostate' because of his frequent changes of creed. He served three English monarchs of various beliefs, and had accepted bribes from the King of France - all for the adornment of Althorp, so he said.

George John, second Earl Spencer (1758-1834), was another; he covered the Tudor brick to make his silver house stand well beside the golden stables built half a century earlier. His sister, the radiant Georgiana Devonshire (1757-1806), "the face without a frown", came home from the roses and raptures of Devonshire House to rest and to teach in the village Sunday school.

In 1919, a curious assortment of people were living in

1

Althorp. There was an elderly, solitary man, living on memories, and a solitary child; no one in between. The rest of the family had grown up and gone. The presence of innumerable and loving servants kept the house alive; the younger ones among them were agitated by numerous courtships, the mature group were strict but sufficiently relaxed to satisfy their thirst mildly whenever possible.

There was not much in the way of human relationships, yet no bad feeling about the lack of them, either then or later. No conscious loneliness marked the child. The house and park took her over: she became part of them and they part of her, and for three years she rested in their stillness. It was as if the *genus loci* knew (as she also knew) that that phase in time would be fleeting.

**\*\*\*\***

# *London*

My early childhood would not stand up to the test of a traditional autobiography. The family unit was unorthodox for me, loosely knit in its components; and the conventional upbringing, about which one reads with riveted attention in other dated memoirs, did not come my way. My mother had died when I was born and there was no single, strong influence; in fact, nothing very expressive in the way of human relationships. I had to find my own fun, and I did.

The continuity was undeviating. Season followed on season, journeys to London came and went. The personalities of the staff never changed; no-one left to 'better themselves', apparently they never succumbed to boredom. They only moved on to marry each other. In describing this perhaps unusual childhood I can, step by step, recapture the deep happiness unconsciously felt by many of my generation, in the precious and simple life we took for granted.

My sister Delia had married, Nannie had also married breaking up the warm nest containing the three of us. After that, it was the Governess in modest command and my father in remote, but total, authority.

To explain but briefly the early years of my life I must introduce my father, who was the regulator of it all. He and I, by that time, had become the only family inhabitants of Althorp. He was too distant and too wretched to be the impresario of it. He never chose the ratio between fun and the intellectual exercises I was put through but he remained an awesome figure. When he ventured into the servants' half of the house, everyone sensed he was there, though none spoke of it. I only knew him in his later life, when he was a broken man. As the only child left of that generation, I am not the most reliable of his children to describe him. I was trained not to get in his way but to tell him of my worries would have been impossible. Yet I would not have changed him. I did not rebel at the restrictions imposed by him; in fact, sometimes I hid behind them.

He had not the Spencer 'feature-squashed' looks. His skin was much darker and, without a doubt, he was very handsome. He wore extraordinary clothes, but they suited him. One of his 'other' war-efforts in 1914-1918 was not to change his enormous high collar for another high collar every day. For daily, when discarding his collars he replaced them with an enlarged version of a tie, which he treated as if it were a collar. His suits never altered; black rough cloth, grey waistcoat greatly in evidence as he never buttoned up his jacket. He rarely walked out of doors, which made his everyday use of black patent leather shoes plausible. His handkerchiefs were wonderful, brought out of his breast pocket with great deliberation.

His conversation was very amusing, most of all when his audience responded to him and laughed (with understanding). When he was in more than usual high spirits, he turned a little wild and inaccurate; mimicking the 'great' he had known many years before. He never discussed those who had sinned; he skated over them in French - "*il était peu chose*" was one of his favourite comments.

My mother, the Hon Margaret Baring, daughter of the first Baron Revelstoke, was the younger by 12 years and had been brought up normally and happily, quite unlike my father's chilly childhood with a widowed mother. They had married when she was 18; she, still with simple plaits and playing the violin beautifully. She had 'fourires'* regularly and seemed to have laughed so much during her short life. She found it difficult to keep up with my father's punctuality, which was extreme, and I am told, she used to rush into dinner late saying "Bobbie, don't fuss".

He cannot have met with anyone so full of spontaneous high spirits before my mother spilt them into his life. It was a great tragedy when she died at my birth. None of her six children ever recovered from this, or ceased to miss her.

****

Having explained the background I will attempt to describe, indeed enhance, the ferment of small excitements which are fun to remember. For me, they have never lost their freshness or their zest.

During the months in London there were unforeseen treats, occurring with suddenness which left no time for days filled with anticipation and excitement. The word 'treat' held magic in those days and, mindful of those whose charisma has never worn thin, I realise that there can hardly be a soul alive today who can recall the giants I was privileged to see. These giants have held their supremacy for over half a century, and must come first.

I think the most memorable of these took place one afternoon, when my father announced that after an early luncheon, we should be walking to St James's Theatre to see a play called 'Daniel'. The title seemed fairly unimportant to him,

* 'fourires' - a Baring expression for uncontrolled laughter.

but he was emphatic that I must remember it always, as I was to see Sarah Bernhardt on the stage. While I hung around the front door, waiting, I noticed that his top-hat was laid out ready, so it must have been a treat for him too! We set out, much before time, and in our appearance we were certainly a curiously-assorted pair.

I remember little of the play except that I had not grown tall enough to see the stage when sitting down, so I stood for the whole performance, without anyone behind complaining that I was breaking the rules.

But suddenly....IT happened; like a shot in the arm. Sarah's voice, powerful, charged with passionate feeling, the recollection of it makes me tingle still. It was impossible not to cry, for no reason other than fear. (My aptitude to cry at the theatre must have begun on that afternoon). Her small, crippled form sitting on a chair was disembodied; there was only the voice, the changes in it extraordinary - the piercing majesty of it when in full volume, and the moments of stillness when the sound dropped nearly to a whisper. For me, at that moment, that voice filled the whole world. I don't remember what she said: it was this feeling of power, something enormous she was tinkering with.

****

Sunday afternoons in London were of unfailing conformity. The schoolroom maid and I climbed on to the upper deck of a number nine bus, an open air experience. When the bus journey was successfully concluded at the Albert Hall, we hurried through the stone passages to our box number 38. I have wondered since whether it opened up new worlds for the kind

*The author's mother: "They had married when she was 18;
she, still with simple plaits and playing the violin beautifully.
She...seemed to have laughed so much during her
short life." She was formerly the Hon Margaret Baring,
second daughter of the first Baron Revelstoke.*

*Lady Adelaide (Delia) Spencer.*
*Her marriage (opposite) to the Hon Sidney Peel took place at*
*St Mary's Church, Brington, in February 1914.*

*Brothers Jack (left), who was to succeed his father as the seventh Earl Spencer in 1922, and Cecil.*

*The Spy cartoon of Lord Althorp (opposite) accompanied an article in a 1907 issue of **Vanity Fair** shortly after he became Lord Chamberlain and had been created a Viscount. Before that he had been an MP and, for 15 years, a successful Liberal Whip in the House of Commons.*

"An Expert in Ceremony"

CHARLES ROBERT, 6™ EARL SPENCER, K.G.
1857—1922
SIR WILLIAM ORPEN, R.A.

*Sir William Orpen's portrait of the sixth Earl.*
*"This picture of my father is supposed to have established his*
*reputation but for me it only demonstrates the distaste felt by*
*the sitter for the whole procedure!"*
*Sir John Sargent's portrait in charcoal appears opposite.*

*Daphne (left) and Calypso Baring at Mothercombe,*
*South Devon, in 1910.*

schoolroom maid, or if she just suffered in silence. These were afternoons listening to heady popular classics sung by the supreme artists of that time, with piano accompaniments. Tetrazzini singing Godard's *Berceuse*, Melba in *Coming through the Rye* and Clara Butt growling through *Abide with Me*. I loved having a lump in my throat and I swallowed all the 'schmaltz' willingly.

The pianist's name must have stayed with me, as when I sat next to him at dinner many years later, I was back in box number 38. He was the great perennial Ivor Newton who was a trifle discomfited to find I was a good bit younger than he was! He became a great friend and, alas, died in 1981.

Another dramatic 'treat', in smarter, less cosy circumstances, but still at the Albert Hall, was hearing Chaliapin. The excitement of seeing him fooling around, playing to the Gallery was tremendous. He threw his white handkerchief all over the place, acted drunk and brought goose flesh out all over us, in his rendering of Russian Army death sagas. To hear him sing *Die Beiden Grenadiere* is totally unforgettable, so unforgettable that I fail to remember the names of other Lieder he sang in the same group!

There were quieter expeditions; two of them, no less remarkable, when I accompanied my father to his 'sittings' with Sargent and Orpen. He was painted by them both, in their studios, in the same year. The sittings were in startling contrast, and so were the differences in feeling and expression on the face of the sitter! Neither artist was English, although both were born English-speaking.

Sargent, a commanding yet homely figure, loosely fitting into his homespun trousers and jacket, murmured unintelligibly throughout the session. He was friendly and reassuring, and fed me with soft, warm biscuits. Orpen dressed as an artist - smocks and all (which was exciting for me as it might have been considered 'Bohemian' by my advanced friends), and was like an insect. He spoke in jerks but remained silent for long, nervous intervals. The rare occasions when he did speak were to comment that I was too young to be my father's daughter! This picture of my father is supposed to have established his reputation but for me it only demonstrates the distaste felt by the sitter for the whole procedure!

The entrance outside Spencer House, and '28' as we called the house next door (it belonged to Aunt Sarah who rented it to us when Spencer House was let), is square and formerly presented great difficulty in turning the horses.

Opposite the front door there is a narrow street, the terminus to the cul-de-sac with dwellings, and one very respectable hotel. Opposite to it there is a concealed passage to Green Park described by Osbert Sitwell thus :-

"I used every day in those weeks to go by the Green Park, and thence into St James's Street, making my way there by means of what had been a dark, narrow passage, pressed between high walls of old and grimy yellow brick but was now open to the air and sky. On one side, below a wall a foot high, I passed every time a floor of white marble with an inlaid circular pattern in the antique manner of porphyry and serpentine a floor now identical in appearance from those from which originally it had been copied a hundred years before, those pavements which had been uncovered by archaeologists in the Roman Forum or in the Golden House of Nero... But what imparted to this floor for me a particular interest arose, I deduce, from my egotism; this was the hall floor of a house in which I had often dined; it was here, standing on these designs in inlaid marble, that the butler and footman had waited deferentially to take the top hats and coats of the guests"

The little passage meant for me an exciting short cut to Gorringes, the life-giving emporium, now extinct.

In the dark evenings of winter, when the passage had been locked by a park official, there were unusual goings-on to watch. Elderly ladies in those days felt safe to stroll about, exercising their dogs alone, before retiring. There was only one hazard for them - a loving couple would come regularly to a roomy triangular corner in between Spencer House and 26 next door. No street lighting stretched as far round and they remained undetected for a long time. It was an ideal venue until a small shaggy grey dog started taking part, followed by its owner, loosely wrapped in a raincoat, who recognised the proceedings as being quite unsuitable to her routine and tried to lure the dog away. A longish struggle followed before they reached the safety of their home and the chastity basket! The loving couple, after two or three skirmishes with the lady and the dog, chose a later time to philander, avoiding the yapping of the dog, so for me, the fun went out of it. I thought the man must have been a butler, because of his bowler hat and dark tidy clothes. Even his gloves looked 'butlerish'. This word has since become extinct, and the meaning of it!

On the other side of the house, the view was extensive over roof tops. I invented a romantic story which went into such a long series that I had to guillotine it. The sound of a violin came from far away, playing Pagliacci and Butterfly as a beginning, and switching fairly soon to the Music Hall favourites of the day. Then a window would open and a figure with hair plaited to her waist leaned out. I convinced myself that it was Rapunzel. The music continued and at its finish they settled down to unhurried conversation, only showing agitation when the window had to be closed; the farewells continued in desperate waving and I never glimpsed the violinist cavalier. It was remote and mysterious, with only my idea clinging to the romance and keeping it alive.

The Underground was banned, on account of the 'DANGER of germs'. Buses were draughty with no protection from the fogs or winds and were as cold as the trains to Northampton, so they passed the rigorous ruling with high marks! It was lucky that they did, as the family 'motor' was seldom allowed the excitement of fresh air. It was cherished as gently as the outmoded horses, in case it suffered from 'metal fatigue'. The mystery I have never solved concerned the bus tickets and the Hyde Park/Green Park chair tickets. The chair tickets were in lovely bright colours and all the children seemed to collect them. They were not allowed to keep the bus tickets; though they were every bit as vivid and attractive; but why were the chair tickets deemed safe, and FREE OF GERMS. How?

When Po-Go sticks appeared in Hamleys, I was the envy of all the Po-Goers who lived in the streets with traffic or pedestrians. I did not suffer from either; it was a perfect Po-Go course. As it was in London, I had to hide the stick, and Po-Go in my tidy clothes with no concessions to leaving off hats, replacing coats with anoraks or anything comfortable. When I crashed one morning, the old gentleman at number 14 wrote me a letter, studiedly formal, commiserating and asking me to tea, "to console you for the hardness of the pavements". I was allowed to go, but he was not asked back, which was worrying. His name was Featherstonhaugh, and my father spent a long time trying to discover the maiden name of his mother, but she was too remote, in more ways than one!

There were no Spencer cousins, so it was fortunate that many of my Baring relations lived in London, breathing unprompted and spontaneous music. We learnt it all together, and executed it in varying degrees of goodness and badness. Playing instruments and speaking French became the strongest recurring themes of our lives when we were children.

One set of cousins stands out vividly: they were beautiful - Daphne and Calypso - and different from all the others, even their mother's knitting was unlike the other aunts'. I knew that the girls' frocks were bought at Lanvin, and it always worried me that when they arrived on foot for tea, they peeled off their white woolly knickers and laid them on the Lanvin coats! It was their mother who made them different - she was American, beautifully turned out and wonderful to look at.

Their drawing room was painted royal blue, exotic and novel compared to our 'off white' one. Their musical parties had taste and expertise. I felt as if I had wandered without warning into another world. How I longed to be like them!

Other cousins, Margaret and Victoria Reid, I met with each day (except Sundays), and their house became a second home to me. I tried to avoid their formidable Scottish nannie, my fear of her increasing with every year. We all shared a family of Welsh music teachers - three brothers, one for the 'cello (the best), one violin (the nicest) and one with least humour, piano. Unlike nowadays, grown-up people never shared music with us or showed knowledgeable interest; it was another green baize door and we played discreetly on the other side of it.

Our musical ensemble was of paramount importance on most afternoons when I was in London. It never occurred to me that we were good, neither did it cross my mind that we were bad! I used to scrape out the part of second violin. We used to tackle whole sonatas and Bach's D minor concerto was often fought over - to get in first.

The cousins, both sets, were brought up more musically than I was. My father used to cry over Victorian songs - one in particular called *Comme on chante à vingt ans*, which had many verses and over-romantic beginnings - but he had no ambition to be knowledgeable about it. He and my mother used to play violin and piano sonatas very often when they first married. The scores of music they used are still ready, waiting for them, as no-one seems to have played them since.

These cousins made quick progress in all the pursuits we followed and to my undying envy were sent to St Paul's School, while I remained with the Governess - destined to become uneducated and moronic.

Dancing classes then were one of the great social amenities, with Miss Vacani the centre of an enormous 'elitist' world. It was not for me; my father could not bring himself to face up to the nonsense of it, so I was despatched to South Kensington, (number 14 bus this time) to Mrs Wordsworth's brand of dancing classes. There I met for the first time the rich professional people; little girls in 'diamanté' shoes, pink silk stockings and overloaded headbands. I thought they were wonderful, was horrified and conscious of my own dowdiness, but they were jolly and fun, in spite of my home-made outfits. Had my father known, it was more snobbish than the alternative class. Mrs Wordsworth had died but was replaced overnight - and her system continued unabated. There were two other 'ladies' and we three suffered agonies when they called us out as 'Lady So-and-So'. Actually there was a little 'Lord' there too, but they never ferreted him out as his name was different from that of his sisters.

I remember girls at that particular class being censured on being well turned out - the Governesses were all against them.

I hated my everyday boots - they were lace-up ones (buttoned ones that needed button hooks were supposed to stop the circulation) and were to strengthen my ankles until I should be tall enough to walk straight then I would be allowed shoes. Duttons was the 'Whites' of shoe shops for little girls. It had grown into such an institution that when it became Peter Yapp and later, even worse, the London Shoe Company, one knew one's youth had disappeared with the bronze dancing pumps, complete with elastic crossed around the ankles, and the elegant subdued gentility of the ladies in Duttons. At last I graduated into shoes, but only for church once a week, so naturally the originality of the treat wore off and anyway I grew out of the shoes!

When all is said and done, my clothes were only intended as coverings, and that is all they were.

It was in Duttons that the Rich New World confronted us one day. The Vanderbilts and their 'confrères', who had led the invasion from the States to Europe were still news and their life styles were noticeable. An American lady with three daughters, all dressed alike, with hats of purple velvet, certainly left a deep impression on Duttons and on me that morning. The daughters were fitted for seven pairs of shoes each, before their mother prepared herself for her own innings. The Invoice Book was not big enough to fill in all the items; boxes for single pairs seemed to jump out from shelves all round the room, and the chauffeur - British - ecologically ignorant of what had hit him, fetched the goods in relays, taking them to the old-fashioned car with precious little 'boot' in which to dispose of them. As they drove away, the boxes made a brighter show than the daughters who were hidden and cramped. I believe the three of them made substantial marriages on this side of the Atlantic; I hope their children went to Duttons to buy their dancing shoes but I doubt if bronze shoes and elastic to match were still in demand by that time. They were a legacy of a particular form of nursery.

**** 

The French class was fun, gales of laughter triggered off by the delightful Professor who was in charge. He was determined to break down the British rigidity and get them laughing. He can have found no difficulty with us. Some of the pupils were taken away fairly soon, as the parents became irritated by the laughter without any background of learning to accompany it. He told us fascinating, terrible stories of French politicians and their ladies of both kinds, and was firm to point out that as they had died such a long time ago, no-one could take umbrage. Equally, no-one could tell if they were true or fantasy.

I remember hearing from another pupil in the French class that she had to leave early because she had to be fitted for her new winter coat and I thought how far fetched that was, with no bearing on my life. The nearest similar situation was when my eldest brother discarded his old red hunting coat and invaluable Mrs Elliot, the linen mender, re-vamped it. I remember also feeling rather hot in the finished coat, but it remained my best full-length, tidiest, fashionable winter coat for quite three years.

Sol-fa was on Tuesday afternoons. An invaluable contribution to anyone's life if they had the dreaded moment coming to them of being asked by a temperamental singer to transpose her song "only a semi-tone", she would say with a beguiling smile, when they knew the difficulty of changing the key a semi-tone is every bit as unpleasant as any other interval. Miss Mills, the brilliant Sol-fa lady, simplified it and made transposing sense. She was fierce, reducing the more sensitive children to tears, and some terrified ones never came back. We wore bags, containing all our music books for the class, held on by an elastic round the waist.

The drawing master wore a skull-cap and a pin-stripe suit, and that was the end of his respectability. He turned out to be leading an unusually intricate 'double' life, regaled to our inquisitive ears by the second in command. One of the class swore she saw him quite often in Paris (where she lived) but he hotly denied ever being there. She said he wore fancy-dress when she saw him. How he continued to feel satisfied was a profound mystery, as the artistic talent shown by the pupils in this particular class was non-existent, and never showed signs of improvement for the whole time I was there.

Mercifully, my world was not limited to the humble package of learning to which I was subjected. My generation was never permitted to 'chip into' an adult conversation; too much so, but we listened to hours of non-small talk. My father, in spite of his solitary life-style, was sufficiently 'au fait' to make the past and present intelligible and fascinating. Among the few friends who appeared for luncheon were Sir Edmund Gosse and the Hon Magdalen (Maggie) Ponsonby, who was also wonderful value. She could not manage her new false teeth, and kept moving them around all through lunch under her napkin. The footmen were convulsed.

It was only during the last few months of my father's life that I was allowed to dine with him alone. We sat at an uncomfortable card table and he gave me a detailed account of the political scene of the 19th century, bringing in the famous names, becoming keen about the personalities he liked, and unreasonably biased against those he did not.

****

The sea-side was the spell-binder in the early part of the twentieth century. Part of the routine was that once a year there was a visit to St Leonards-on-Sea. When the time for this came round, Mr and Mrs Graham of 81 Marina were our hosts. The weather changed simultaneously with our arrival - for the worse. I was never permitted even to take off my socks, or those dreadful hats, bound to my head forever by elastic. Perhaps it was for the best that there was never a heatwave! We must have always been there in the less smart season as the only people I remember were distinctly elderly.

Mr Graham had two 'unbendable' fingers on his right hand. What held my attention was watching to see what he could carry with the remaining two, as the thumb no longer counted. The Grahams introduced me to Scottish porridge (with Jersey cream and brown sugar) so overwhelmingly strong that I begged to be allowed to leave it. I have never found porridge, even in Scotland, to compare with the severity of that particular brand. One year a friend accompanied us as a companion for me; we both had measles. The plan collapsed in failure when she sobbed noisily from home-sickness and her parents refused to fetch her home.

81 Marina smelt like the house of shut doors so powerfully described by Tolstoy but the Grahams, coming from the north, were fresh-air fiends! So perhaps the smell must have been that

the carpets were seldom cleaned. There were Pierrot Shows along the front, and entertainments galore on the beach itself. An old gentleman who was wheeled about in a bath-chair (as they were called then) suffered from elephantiasis of the nose. It was wrapped in a colossal napkin, and for ages I thought it was a beard, like the Spencer Red Earl's. The old gentleman was well-known, was there year after year and he and I became great friends. There were many friends of all ages, lots of little girls in scarlet berets, like mine - I met them too year after year on the promenade at St Leonards!

****

One visit, which strangely made a little history for me, when staying for a party in Northampton, was when I met Grape Nuts for the first time. In other houses I had come across beetroot, ice-cream and macaroni-cheese, all of them disowned at home but which have remained my favourites. For this particular party, the only new item I was allowed to embellish my appearance was a pale blue velvet band for my hair lined with elastic. Some white net had been lying about the linen-room for a long time, so had some 'jap-silk'. So Mrs Elliot, the same invaluable linen mender, ran them both up thoroughly, and luckily they pointed in the same direction. A sash was necessary and there was the very thing! A length of wide satin ribbon used for my elder sister's 'bust bodice', (they were not 'bras' in those days) was joined in several places and off I went. If the object of the exercise was to embellish my appearance and make me more 'partyfied' - it failed!

Clothes panic happened only once, but for a day it created hard words and caused hurt feelings. I was invited to a Royal party for young people. Sophisticated and trendy relations were brought in to give a solemn opinion of what I ought to wear, and they took five minutes to throw the poor Governess and her choice out of the window. The second outfit, surprisingly, was duller than the first.

The one visit of consequence I made before I was grown-up was to Southill, the home of the Whitbreads, and this time it was a REAL party. Southill was built by the same architect as Althorp, which made an immediate 'rapport' as there was definite similarity between them. I was surprised to feel so much at home in the passages! There the resemblance came to a halt, for Southill had a rare and gracious 'chatelaine' to keep it beautiful and 'les petits soins' were done to perfection. I liked the silk bed-spreads best but it was all a feast to my uninitiated eye. The Ball was joyful, full of happy junior teenagers with the daughter of the house leading a graceful 'Cotillon'. I realised then with indescribable sadness how much my father had to struggle against cruel circumstances bereft of a wife. Mrs Warren and Mrs Reeves, the cook, tried their best but they would have considered the introduction of small inessentials silly, perhaps ungodly, certainly embarrassing. So Althorp would have to remain austere (never unloved) until the next Lady Spencer made it feminine again, and filled it with her own special personality, which indeed she did.

One of my odder recollections concerns a 'two-seater' convertible Singer car. My eldest brother dropped in to the schoolroom one evening, in his Life Guards uniform, and suggested taking me for a drive in his new 'motor'.

It was regarded as an outsize treat by everyone but myself. I was appalled that I should be thrown to the slaughter, allowed to go out with an amateur. No-one but a professional ought to be in charge (even though it was broad daylight); surely this was the first rule of safety? I felt as if I was being forced into a space capsule with a learner pilot! I had never seen a car without a peaked cap in it; sometimes there were two, if there was a boy on the box.

My legs went weak as I climbed in and I remember intoning "Gentle Jesus, meek and mild" very quietly the whole way round central London. I was amazed that we arrived home safely in one piece and, in my judgement, my brother had exercised hitherto unrecognised expertise.

To round off life in London, it is impossible to forget the Coronation of George V, as I saw it at three years old (nearly four) - the earliest memory that I am able to pinpoint.

I remember being squeezed to a pulp in a stand. I was conscious, above all else, of wearing stockings for the first time. They were bronze and much too hot for midsummer but I was mightily proud of them and I had to show them to the person sitting beside me. Disruption raged after I pulled out my leg to display them, as it was impossible to get the leg back. There was just not room. It must have been at that moment that my father, as Lord Chamberlain, passed in his gold coach, wilting visibly, until he caught sight of my twisted posture and leg obviously out of control, when the 'wilt' on his face gave way to horror. As far as I remember, there were no comments, no reprisals.

# *Althorp*

After weeks of longing, the moment of seeing Althorp again was always dramatic; we had arrived!

I would sniff the familiar atmosphere inside the house, absorb the indefinite deep green of the Park and the stillness of the proud oaks. I went through these swift appraisals before most of those who had taken their courage in both hands and travelling by train were coaxed, sometimes forced, towards their beds. This was the prescribed remedy to offset the ordeal of a journey lasting two whole hours! Those two hours were mesmerised by watching the delightful advertisements encouraging everyone to use Hall's Distemper and no other. Even Bovril had not yet invaded the advertisements on all the railway lines in the country, those two indefatigable young men in sole possession of their ladder, plodding along in the same direction in every few fields.

The even tenor of our routine at Althorp would begin now that the move had been successfully undertaken. There would be no companionship of musical cousins, not many glimpses of outside culture, but Althorp was the resting place where people felt integrated, perhaps complete.

Soon after our arrival there would be May Day festivities, starting with songs at the back door, the whole porch festooned with baskets, one to each singer, overflowing with primroses. The songs had their origins far, far back. In the evening, dancing round the maypole on one of these auspicious occasions I ruined the complex set dance by going right instead of left. The whole thing had to begin again and I was scorned for the remainder of the evening.

There were not 'treats' as such at Althorp; there were minor privileges to break the monotony of the routine. One of these was staying up later than usual for family prayers, my time then chiefly spent in sticking my finger into a small hole in the damask kneeler to see how much it could become a bigger hole by the end of the second prayer. The female staff filed in, with their lace caps readjusted by enormous pins, only moments before the time to muster. They were rounded up by Mrs Warren, the formidable housekeeper; likewise the male contingent, with Mr Evans (Evvie) brought up the rear.

Mrs Warren, known as 'Mars' by her subordinates, was not greatly loved. She wore a cap decorated with black velvet, and wore it with great 'chic', and there was no question, ever, of an apron or duster anywhere near her person. She was not famous for her natural compassion, though on one occasion she moved quickly and successfully to the protection of one of the senior members of her staff, the head laundry maid. The laundry maids lived alone in a cottage, ruled over firmly by Annie, the head laundry maid, who was no taller than 4ft 8ins. She wore a cameo brooch almost as large as herself, with the Lord's Prayer written on it.

The footmen, in their separate wing, were never taken on unless they measured over six feet in height. Mrs Warren did not approve of Annie being teased by members of the opposite sex (she was actually photographed with the footmen) and was bent on rationalising the situation. She was determined to find a fleet of midget laundry maids! I doubt if her writing ability was very pronounced but she must have written a great many letters (no telephone to expedite the delays), for she succeeded in adjusting the discrepancy between Annie, her underlings and all the outsize footmen. They were proudly photographed all together, the laundry maids looking like Florence in the *Magic Roundabout*. Someone suggested that the laundry girls being too small might be in danger in case they got caught in the narrow confines of the extraordinary drying horses, which were exciting to ride in, but I was never aware of this happening. The type of drying horse there is very difficult to explain - there was a distinct danger of being shut inside them for ever - a question of the latch going 'out-of-order' which happened frequently.

Two special events dominated us all on the estate for months, the visit of King George and Queen Mary for the Army manoeuvres in the Park, and the coming of age of my eldest brother. Both took place in 1913.

They were magnificent occasions, but so hopelessly mixed in my memory that they became amalgamated. There was the same marquee, the same fireworks and the same strawberry fool brought by Nannie's sister to wake me up in time for the 10 o'clock revels. I do remember dancing a waltz with an enormously tall man called Sir Hill Childs, and that I wore bronze shoes. Surely, it was the coming of age, as I would have never been allowed to dance with a man of any size in the presence of the Monarch?

Bugles sounded all day during the manoeuvres; bustle and people everywhere. The face of my world changed for the time being and the uniforms made me believe that I was indeed inside that masterpiece, Fortescue's *The Drummer's Coat*, which I was reading with such joy at the time.

The coming-of-age was younger, more in the style of a chaperoned tennis party. Straw hats more than brass hats and certainly more speeches! However, nothing was grander or more beautiful than the balls for the tenants and estate workers

*"Two special events dominated us all on the estate for months, the visit of King George and Queen Mary for Army manoeuvres in the Park, and the coming of age of my eldest brother. Both took place in 1913. They were magnificent occasions…"*

*Still on Army manoeuvres: the King and Queen meet the Pytchley Hounds, and Queen Mary, accompanied by Earl Spencer, planting an oak tree to commemorate the Royal visit. These photographs come from the family's albums, and the mark on the photograph above is due to an overlap with another picture.*

*The author's mother at her desk. On the wall behind her are portraits of three of her children, Jack, Delia and Cecil, brothers and sister of Margaret Douglas-Home.*

in the big dining room. I remember seeing my father wearing tight, white kid gloves, dancing a Quadrille with Charlotte Spencer's French maid. She was a trifle bewildered at the British speed, carried on against a background of bowing and curtsying. It was the only time I had seen my father hurry! I was eligible for only one ball before they were inevitably, and sadly, given up because of the aftermath of the 1914-18 War.

Life continued with occasional excitements. One afternoon there was a rush to the front of the house to see a small but determined aeroplane circling around, not in distress, perhaps merely inquisitive. We were convinced that it was the first aircraft to pioneer a route as far as Northamptonshire, and that may well have been true.

The clock in the Stables affected my life in precisely the same way as it did to everyone living in the Park. Relentless in its accounting for every quarter, it built a shape out of the day. Authority had to confirm and promote meals at certain hours, unpopular to some, but there was The Clock summoning, exhorting and certain of obedience. When I hear it now, I find myself moving in the same direction as I would have done all those years ago. No-one needed wrist watches, or any other kind, until they were leaving the Park. Some people found the constant register of time a tyranny but I was happy to obey The Clock.

I can think of two people who relied entirely on The Clock, for their well-being. One was old Mr Worley, known as 'Dot and Carry One', as his slow progression was of a distinctly fitful variety. The Clock told him when to turn in another direction and his umbrella advised him when to take cover; one of the carters was always on the look-out for him and would whisk him, grumbling noisily, to Mrs Tufton who lived in the

Lodge nearest to Little Brington, where he lived. I wonder if his spirit goes on walking!

The other person was more robust. She had settled her fate to the most comfortable method for her to deal with. Her name was Mrs Winn, and she helped in the kitchen. She may have been too rotund to bicycle as I never saw her using one. Every afternoon at four o'clock she emerged from the back door and walked very fast, her head down, to the main road leading to the village. She appeared to be weighed down, on both sides, by bursting carrier bags. They were usually new ones, and always bursting! Off she went apparently unaffected by her life-size burden;  being short of stature, she had to grapple with the carrier bags practically touching the ground all the time. It turned into a game trying to guess what was so regularly (every day) in Mrs Winn's carrier bags. I missed seeing her four o'clock walk home after my father died, when she no longer came to help in the kitchen, and was worried that she might suffer financially from her greatly reduced income.

The First War is a hazy memory, except for the dread of accompanying my father to the station to see off the boys and men. They were my friends, the gardeners who had broken the see-saw with me and the grooms who had concealed the fact they still held the leading rein when I was frightened. All the estate, bearing the village names I knew so well, with their wives and sweethearts, silent and whitefaced. And, in what seemed like a very short time, going with him again to visit the bereaved relations. The dairyman's only son was the worst, his mother unable to stem the terrible paroxysms of crying. After the first weeks, she sat and gazed from an upstairs window, and for years I only remember her doing just that. I never heard of her walking again. The little commemorative grave stones put up by my father are still on the garden wall, half hidden by the virginia creeper.

An avalanche of wounded soldiers in their pale blue uniforms descended on Althorp, slept in all the estate houses and stables, strolled and sat about the gardens and grounds. There was one who I have remembered. His name was Percy Cattermole, and obviously he was more deeply wounded than most of the others as he stayed longest, much to the delight of my sister. There was also a Captain Brown in khaki, whom she clung to. I recall that my father took exception to Captain Brown, but grew fond of Percy Cattermole.

**\*\*\*\***

The other change brought about by the War was the introduction of parlour-maids to replace the six-footers. The gardeners were never replaced and nor were the grooms. The house staff was halved and no more schoolroom maid for me, which landed me in the local Girl Guide company to learn the sensible skills I should have started much sooner: darning, knitting, mending my own punctures, bathing any baby who might appear unannounced and, best of all, dancing the hornpipe at tremendous speed.

Our Girl Guides cannot have been a usual group. We were very mixed with country folk, Northampton folk, and 'just come folk'. Some had been reluctant to join when the Company was in the process of forming. I remember the yearly Camp not being a 'happy' success, but the weekly sessions held together provided for me the strongest and really the only excitement in a long week.

I loved what we did even more than whom I did it with! And

spending five desperately energetic hours with people of my own age was amazing. The elation would continue into supper, after they had left me, when I was upgraded from biscuits and milk to bread and milk! Very significant!

I vaguely remember bathrooms being installed - there was only one when we arrived but 16 when my father died - and 'loos' springing into being all over the house, little slits converted, some of them almost too small, though they all had wooden seats which made them high class!

In the War I worried over the yet untested parlour-maids. My first thought was what would they be given for Christmas presents? Material for a dress, as for the maids, or cash, like the men? It was awful that they were neither one thing nor the other. The beauty who arrived first was too much of a classical type to be at home with the few masculine figures left. The second little plump one was off to a swift start and married the second footman almost at once.

Christmas remained important, the house agitated by many people moving with a sense of purpose from one end of the house to the other. Valets waiting outside gentlemen's bedroom doors, or carrying pressed trousers towards those doors, but inevitably they had to vanish as the later generations would not have had enough clothes for anyone to 'wait outside'.

The stage would be set up in the Long Library at Althorp and the Baring cousins would arrive to act French plays, and to play quartets to anyone unwise enough to come and listen.

The rehearsals were great fun when (and it was 'when') the school-boy members of the cast turned up. I believe we sang songs too. I was the youngest and thought everything unblemished and wonderful. It seems extraordinary that we used to give performances to the house staff - perhaps they dared not refuse!

For months on end there would be no companionship with cousins or any glimpse of outside 'intelligentsia' calling on my father, but there was time to rest the soul and rise refreshed at Althorp. It was easy to look, then read, then look again. But life was not all solitary by any means. There was syrup of figs every Friday night, administered by the butler Evvie, who arrived upstairs in his shirt sleeves, having finished his more important duties elsewhere. There was skating on the Round Oval, the pond at Althorp, with chestnuts roasted on an enormous bonfire. Jam-making in the still room went on the whole summer long, and the warm, delicious smell seemed to spread to the farthest bedrooms.

Riding was indispensable to life at Althorp. The Pytchley Hounds came for the whole summer; hunting and meets were popular topics of conversation at all times of the year. In the time of the 'Red Earl' the stables had housed as many as 100 horses. The amusing thing as far as I was concerned was that no concession was made to provide suitable clothes for me in which to ride. I wore what I was already in, never saw jodhpurs or breeches of any kind until I was out of my teens and a mature, practically married horsewoman!

If one was bored on the way up to bed, there was always someone in the act of lowering the flag. If it happened to be Fred Manning, so much the better as he was loaded with acid drops, and there would be a long chat of unusual information about his glamorous daughters, who enlivened the back yard enormously, much to the disapproval of Mrs Warren. Fred was meant to hoist it again in the morning but usually forgot until it was afternoon.

If one felt the need to laugh with anyone, there was always Tom Irons, shiny with coal dust and everyone's favourite. He wore an apron of the thickest leather (meant to be indestructible); I wonder what happened to it, it could not have worn out? His task was to shift trolleys of coal on to the primitive lifts specially built for the purpose that went from the cellars to the top floor. He was pleased to be waylaid and would oblige with cheerful willingness to recite the alphabet backwards, a contribution to literature of which he was justly proud. He did it fluently with telling gesticulation and it was difficult to extricate oneself until he had finished. When asked why he did this so often his answer was, "it takes me mind off me trouble". What trouble no-one ever knew, except that he had always suffered from bad feet.

There were red-bearded farm labourers, looking so like some of the sitters in the family portraits that the continuity seemed even more complete. The village Scout Master was one of the labourers. He had no beard, but the hair on his head was of the tell-tale tawny red and, oddly, his bare knees were thick with it. He could have sat for so many of those country Spencers on the walls with his knees covered, of course!

My Nannie's father and my Nannie herself also showed a striking resemblance to many of the red-haired Spencers. In our walks and drives outside the Park, I was constantly taken for her daughter, we looked so alike. It never occurred to me then, it only has now!

As early as I can remember, there was a 'spooky' element in the house which was a thrill tinged with real fear. It was the old 'parrot maid', a legacy from Charlotte Spencer who collected parrots as other people collected stamps - far too many for hygiene or for comfort, even for the parrots. Her name was Mary Chowler and she had seen 50 years' service at Althorp, in what capacity I do not know. She shuffled and hobbled around, dressed in Charlotte Spencer's cast-off clothes. The skirt was pinned around her and sometimes she wore the discarded evening gowns. She had been given a suite on the second floor of the house with thick curtains on the outside doors to keep out the terrible parrot smell, which refused to go away! Her voice had become identical with the screams of the parrots. Her hats were of the large summer variety with wreaths of flowers falling off them. She was a disturbing and tragic figure. I wondered what she had been like as a young woman; could she have ever been young?

****

Our travelling never varied for any reason and it kept to a routine. In my childhood I had never heard of the Costa Brava across the sea. My Costa Brava was in Norfolk, at North Creake, the estate bought 200 years earlier by Sarah, Duchess of Marlborough. Each year, there it was, ready for us to wake it up from dreamless winter sleep - The Shooting Box.

A holiday spirit prevailed from the minute we arrived, also the feeling of freedom because of its smallness after Althorp. The heavy hand of discipline seemed remote, sometimes non-existent. The heads of departments had been left behind, leaving the juniors to laugh and sing as they worked, and go out a lot with friends they had been inclined to hide at Althorp.

I remember feeling unanchored at first without 'Evvie', in case I should break my collar bone or need Syrup of Figs. Both operations he had supervised with authority.

Before the long journey from Althorp began, there was a concession to informality in that the solitary footman who would accompany us was excused the wearing of livery from the waist upwards. On top of the black livery trousers, a tweed jacket of a personal choice was allowed, sometimes rather gaudy. The tweed jacket was a sure sign that the Norfolk migration was in motion. Migration it certainly was. Our departure from Althorp was fairly spectacular. We travelled by train in a special coach, sandwiched between two ordinary ones. One hoped the Norfolk light would not be far away, once the train shunted off. It was this one coach which carried the humans and paraphernalia all the way to the station at Burnham Market.

Our personal luggage was peculiar and considerable; musical instruments, my father's scarlet dressing-gown which was the opposite to a travelling one, and lived in a trunk by itself; saddles, harness and strangest of all, two ponies. We were not initiated into Boat life, which was perhaps a blessing. I believe the previous generation to ours brought a pair of Jersey cows! It was not unlike piling up the car and loading the trailer to their utmost as we do now, but we arrange it more comfortably and with less bureaucracy. After an endless journey, we paused on the platform at Fakenham, with only a few more miles to inch along!

North Creake brings to my mind the Bishop of Thetford. Since his official retirement, he had become an institution in this neighbourhood. He was uncanny with our arrival in the timing of his first call to us. He anticipated the boiled egg at tea, again, a build-up of protein, after the unpredictability of a train journey. He also loved the white painted chairs with red bobbles on the back as much as I did. Every year, he showed his joy in finding them still in situ. I discovered that he was Sybil Thorndike's uncle fairly lately.

The Shooting Box alas is no longer standing.   It was a

*On holiday: The Shooting Box (above), at North Creake in Norfolk,*
*which alas no longer stands, and St Leonards-on-Sea, Sussex.*

*Althorp (above), noted John Evelyn when he visited in 1788,*
*"is a noble uniformed pile".*
*Below: Dallington House near Northampton,*
*where the very early years were spent.*

*The fifth Earl Spencer, the 'Red Earl'. He was succeeded by his half-brother Viscount Althorp, the author's father, in 1910.*

*"My Aunt Sarah paid us regular twice-yearly visits, bringing with her a veritable retinue of her nurse, her maid, and her Pekinese, Biba. She was half-sister to my father, which lack of 'wholeness' appeared to make him distant towards her."*

*Two portraits of brother Jack: The picture opposite, in which he is accompanied by the author and his daughter, who later became Lady Anne Wake-Walker, was taken in January 1923 at a meet of the Pytchley shortly after he had become the seventh Earl Spencer.*

*Lady Margaret Spencer at the age of 18.*

casualty of the 1939 War, requisitioned to house the Services. Unfortunately, the funds necessary for its restoration were unavailable. The gate, the stable yard and the wall backing onto the road are still standing.

Following a small piece I wrote for the North Creake parish magazine, an anonymous lady sent a charming memoir of the Shooting Box during the War. She kindly agreed to let me include it in my memoir.

## THE SHOOTING BOX

"It seemed such a long journey, riding one dark September evening in the back of an open truck, from Fakenham station to the Shooting Box in North Creake.

Not until the next morning did I have my first glimpse of Norfolk from the big bay window of the bedroom I was to share for the next three years.

Unlike our earlier writer who journeyed to the Shooting Box for annual holidays, it was from this beautiful house I and many other Land Army girls left each morning early with our tools and a tin of sandwiches, (the usual chocolate spread and cucumber) to do many jobs we were called to do in the fields, under the careful eye of our drivers, Sam and Gus.

It was a fascinating old house we returned to each evening, with its row of servant bells, stone floored kitchen and dark, damp laundry room.

Our sitting room had a large fire-place which glowed with burning logs on cold winter evenings.

Fig trees grew up the walls outside. Stables in the courtyard; how I would stand and try to imagine the fine ponies and horses they once housed.

After our essential evening chores, washing, ironing, *etc* we played records, the few we had, (no TV in those days for us), or played table-tennis in the large hallway.

Some curled up in one of the few armchairs to read a book or with a pad and pen to write home to our families.

Our main occupation was keeping out of Matron's way. Although her bark was worse than her bite, she was very strict with us.

How sad I was to see the Shooting Box demolished, the garden so deserted and overgrown now. Just a few primroses blooming there the other day when I looked over the wall.

Remembering such a lovely old house is remembering the many friendships formed there, so many years ago."

Mornings were for bicycling when everyone else was busy. I was free, free! No lark sang in those Norfolk fields with greater exultation than I, riding alongside them on my bike. Were all those September days as golden as I remember them? Best of all, there was no bed-time ruling, no-one to scold; living in the sun all day and, of a summer's evening, dreaming in the brilliance of the setting sun which drenched the stubble fields with light.

Memories of my childhood holidays there are strong. The stream in the garden, with its dangerous bridges which took a month of progressive courage and powers of navigation, to negotiate. I recall the picnics in the waggonette* every day, picking early blackberries, or paddling in the telescopic, invisible sea at Holkham. The biggest treat was to shop in

* Waggonette: a horse-drawn carriage; similar to a trap or dog cart - holds six to eight people.

Fakenham, exploring woods and lonely roads on the way, always returning by way of Nellie Durrant's cottage in South Creake. She lay by her window, bed-ridden, making table-cloths and pillow slips with a minute crochet hook. She gave me a table-cloth as a wedding present, still in my possession and brought out on best occasions. I have never discovered if her disability had been caused by an accident or whether she was born with it. She was wholly and immensely happy.

****

Few people came to stay at Althorp; they had to like something special about it to want to come. Of these, Edmund Gosse was the nicest, the funniest and the only one who never lost touch between his visits. He was one of my father's closest friends and they wrote to each other regularly twice a week for a number of years. I doubt if they even used Christian names to each other.

"Dear Gosse" and "Dear Friend" were the usual modes of address they used in their correspondence. My correspondence with him began when he asked me to send him reports of my father's health. He was especially fond of the dog, a greyhound; describing her eyes as bulls eyes which had been well-sucked. This comment reduced the footmen to helpless giggles at lunch, when he said it for the first time! I saw him once walking in the garden at dusk, declaiming loudly, almost with violence, and have wondered so often what plagued him with such force as he appeared so disturbed. I was frightened by it for months.

My Aunt Sarah paid us regular twice-yearly visits, bringing with her a veritable retinue of her nurse, her maid and her

Pekinese, Biba. She was half-sister to my father, which lack of 'wholeness' appeared to make him distant towards her.

Every third day she stayed in bed but in the intervals of her not being horizontal, she was very dear to me indeed. She had told us that she enjoyed dancing the Lancers* more than any of the other dances. Every gentleman in her 'set' had asked her to marry him. There must have been eight of them at least!

One of Aunt Sarah's legs was shorter than the other; broken in the mist of antiquity. It was the cause of her relations making her into an invalid. She beat us all at Racing Demon until the last year of her life; when she no longer won, we then knew she was ill unto death.

She made me recite the 23rd Psalm to her every morning, and then stay quiet until she gave me the all clear "...to begin ticking like a taxi" again, as she called it. Aunt Sarah was the last Poyntz descendant left. Her Pekinese, Biba, was left to the nurses when Aunt Sarah died and must have survived her by many years. When the little dog eventually died the nurse wrote to my brother to say she was sending Biba BY POST to be buried on the island of the Round Oval, with the other family dogs. The corpse took weeks to arrive during which time of suspense my brother was too nervous to open any parcel. The weakness of his case was that he did not know the likely post mark!

Two great bonuses of my childhood were, first, the arrival of a cousin, Bess Bigham, to do 'lessons' with me and live in for the terms. She was beautiful, with esoteric intelligence. I remember well an essay she wrote which was strikingly unusual and attractive. I wonder now, though, if the whole enterprise

---

* The 'Lancers' was a popular country dance, sets of 16 people, eight men, eight ladies. We danced it at all our parties.

was a time of wretchedness for her; I look back with shame to remember how little I did to counteract her homesickness. Whether the breadth of intelligence was too unnerving for the limitations of the Governess (Bess would answer back with courage when it was necessary) or whether the ambience was too different from her cultured and happy home life, I never knew. At all events, she did not stay long and I was the poorer for her leaving.

The second bonus fell on me without warning; almost as if nobody had thought of it at all. I was suddenly being measured for a gym-tunic and prepared for entry to the Northampton Secondary School for Girls, admittedly only on Tuesdays, but what a breakthrough. Nothing that has happened since has ever brought with it such a feeling that the gates of paradise must be opening, and that the future would be golden.

The day was not long enough to hold such excitement. The following weeks I was allowed the independence of bicycling to Althorp station to catch the early train to Northampton, wearing on my head the sum total of my ambition... a STRAW BOATER. This bonus was a complete success.

Outside the Park, there lay two holy places; at least, they were for me. Harlestone Heath, a mysterious forest (just too far for bicycling with picnic accoutrements hanging on the front handlebars) but infinitely ghostly, the fir trees gently sighing, and a feeling that the tread of the dinosaur was padding silently around every corner. It was a dark green deep forest, with needles dropping to form a carpet from the pines... There was the timelessness of silence, the invisibility of no panorama. Someone usually brought a ball, planning rounders or some other exercise but it was never in use. It was a place to think and wonder. We went there in the governess cart; no-one was allowed to call it by that name, as the Governess herself was outraged by the word. She had to be known as 'the Lady who teaches', so Dog Cart it was, and the dogs were not allowed to mind! The Barouche was the most fun. The hood had the same fittings as my dolls' pram.

And Nobottle Wood, bicycling up a pebbly lane, plunging into the green glades and staying there until a crescent moon made magic of it all. It was called Newbottle in the Domesday Book and surely must have been transparently innocent then, as it is now, with sunlight peering through the leaves and the warm rain of May quietly refreshing the green rides which were bound by the shallow ditches. Those ditches started reflecting the sunset in their puddles on the West of the wood, only completing the cycle just before the East sank into darkness.

Spring does not come to Nobottle Wood in Tolstoyan fashion, breaking winter overnight with deafening cascades and torrents hurling themselves down the hills. The advance of the year is in order, and its spring arrives at the time it is expected, heralded by birdsong and pussy-willows. My father used to make the same comment each year: "le vert tendre ne dure qu'un instant". It was indeed a miracle and transformed the beeches and oaks into haunting beauty.

On milky afternoons, when the sun refused to come out, I would tidy up the primroses by lifting their heads above the undergrowth, where they were being steadily suffocated. There were bluebells, too, with no individuality compared with the cuckoo flower or stitchwort, in spite of their superior numbers. The small orchis seeded themselves on the edge of the wood, and bloomed later hoping to please. They were all indelibly printed on my 'spring' mind - and Nobottle stayed as a Spring Festival; there was never a disappointment in seeing the wild flowers become low-powered and fractional in the summer months as our visits then were rare.

It is many, many years since I heard the nightingales in Nobottle; it would not be possible to forget the beauty of the bird song in amongst the trees lit by a midsummer moon. It is one of the most fulfilled of my memories.

The House, the Stables, the Park, the old Nursery and the Servants Hall; when I was away, I called these places my 'bastions'. They held individuals; they were bound to me through the fact of their being solid, touchable, sometimes protective, sometimes severe. They could tell me which way to go, they had been there so much longer than I had. My routine continued quietly and the days grew out of each other.

****

The summer of 1922 was particularly beautiful - it seemed to give so much. I and my household friends all knew that my father's death would be the natural climax to our way of life and jolt us sideways. I told myself (and confided in one of the young housemaids) that to alter one's life style could not be a very difficult thing to do but when the moment arrived for me to do just that, it was crippling. No certainty, whichever way one looked, no rightful niche belonging beyond any question to me. I was not anybody's daughter any more. I would lose my friendships on the estate as they probably would move on. Time alone could sort out these problems.

I was sent to school in Paris as soon as it could be arranged; there I stayed learning French Literature and studying music in an entirely different way. I stayed in France for two and a half years and then returned to Spencer House, ready for my coming-out ball, with a dress from Molyneux (costing £15). To dance a Viennese waltz and wait for the dawn of a May morning meant that I had grown-up!

The magic of that particular ball lay in the beauty of the Ballroom, the surprise of a large garden and the fact that we lived in it, therefore not used only for the one occasion. Everything before, during and after was done by our own much-loved people. That made it a family affair; the staff shared it and talked about 'our' dance for months afterwards.

I remember hearing one of the footmen telling the housemaid that the Duchess of Portland's tiara "cannot have been cleaned for a long time"!

Yes, magic there was, in spite of the plethora of tail-coats, and the excessive amount of inherited jewellery! No-one unmarried over the age of twenty-four was invited (not even relations). The older 'marrieds' in their diamonds brought the romance to the magic, halfway through the fleeting spring night. It stayed 'special' for a long time, in the memory of all who were there.

When Marshall, the brilliant pianist, left the piano and his band, wrapped in their tweed coats, disappeared, the shutters of the Ballroom windows were opened and there was the new day with bird song from Green Park.